CONTENTS

ARCADE

Words and Music by DUNCAN DE MOOR,
WOUTER HARDY, JOEL SJOO
and WILL KNOX

Moderate Pop Ballad

COVER ME IN SUNSHINE

Words and Music by MAUREEN McDONALD
and AMY ALLEN

BAD HABITS

Words and Music by ED SHEERAN,
JOHNNY McDAID and FRED GIBSON

BEAUTIFUL MISTAKES

Words and Music by ADAM LEVINE,
MATTHEW MUSTO, JACOB KASHER HINDLIN,
ANDREW GOLDSTEIN, JOSEPH KIRKLAND
and MEGAN PETE

Male: It's beau-ti-ful, it's bit-ter-sweet; you're like a bro-ken home to me. I
ev-'ry day gets worse for me. I

take a shot of mem-o-ries and black out like an emp-ty street. I
take a break, I cut you off to keep my-self from look-ing soft. I

Additional Lyrics

Rap 1: You did me wrong 'cause I let you.
Usually, I like my situations beneficial.
Doin' something different, got me lookin' stupid.
The only way I'm comin' back to you is if you dream it lucid.

Rap 2: Prove it. If you made a promise, then keep it.
Why you wanna lie and then get mad? I don't believe it.
But really, I was doin' just fine without ya,
Lookin' fine, sippin' wine, dancin' on club couches.

Rap 3: Baby, why you wanna lose me like you don't need me?
Like I don't block you and you still try to reach me?
How you figure out how to call me from the TV?
You're runnin' outta chances, and this time I mean it.

BEGGIN'

Words and Music by BOB GAUDIO
and PEGGY FARINA

Slowly, very freely

Put your lov- in' hand out, ba- by, _____ 'cause I'm beg - gin'.

Moderately fast, steadily

I'm beg - gin', beg - gin' you, _____

DEJA VU

Words and Music by OLIVIA RODRIGO,
DANIEL NIGRO, JACK ANTONOFF,
TAYLOR SWIFT and ANNIE CLARK

place; I found it first. __ I made the jokes __ you tell to her __ when she's with you. Do

you get dé - jà vu when she's with you? _____ Do you get dé - jà vu, __ hm? __

Do you get dé - jà vu, huh?

Do you

GOOD 4 U

Words and Music by OLIVIA RODRIGO,
DANIEL NIGRO, HAYLEY WILLIAMS
and JOSH FARRO

Driving Pop Rock

(Ah.)
Well, good for you, I guess you moved on real-ly eas-i-ly.
You found a new girl and it on-ly took a cou-ple weeks.
Re-mem-ber when you said that you want-ed to give me the world? _____
(Ah.) _____

To Coda ⊕

THE GOOD ONES

Words and Music by GABBY BARRETT,
ZACHARY KALE, EMILY FOX LANDIS
and JAMES McCORMICK

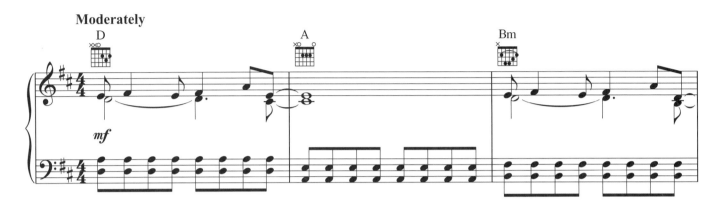

Moderately

He's a phone call to his par-ents, he's a Bi-ble by the bed. He's the

T-shirt that I'm wear-ing, he's the song stuck in my head. He's sol-id and he's stead-y like the

HOLD ON

Words and Music by JUSTIN BIEBER,
JON BELLION, ANDREW WATT,
WALTER DE BACKER, ALI TAMPOSI,
LUIZ BONFA and LOUIS BELL

LEVITATING

Words and Music by DUA LIPA,
STEPHEN KOZMENIUK, CLARENCE COFFEE JR.
and SARAH HUDSON

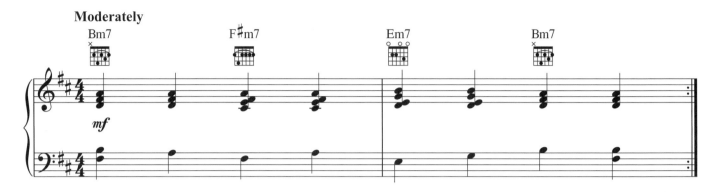

LEAVE THE DOOR OPEN

Words and Music by BRUNO MARS,
DERNST EMILE, CHRISTOPHER BRODY BROWN
and BRANDON PAAK ANDERSON

* Recorded a whole step lower.

LOST CAUSE

Words and Music by BILLIE EILISH O'CONNELL
and FINNEAS O'CONNELL

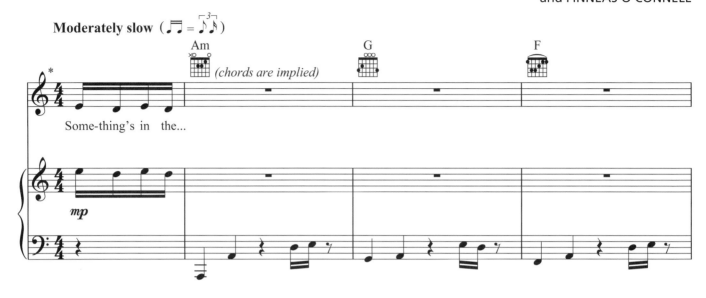

Moderately slow

Recorded a half step higher.

YOUR POWER

Words and Music by BILLIE EILISH O'CONNELL
and FINNEAS O'CONNELL

Moderately

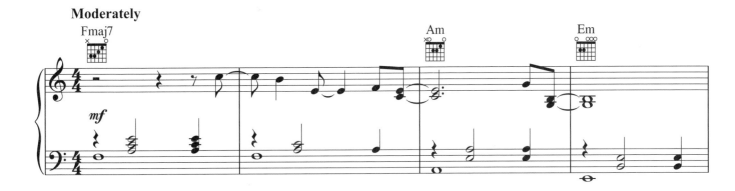

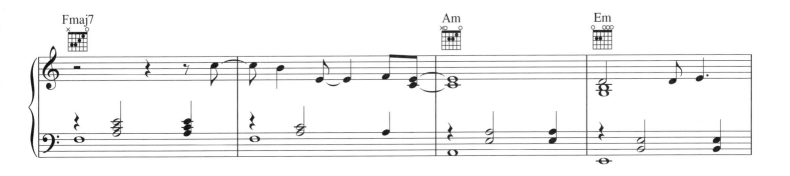

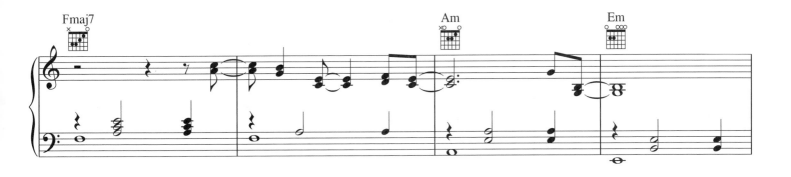

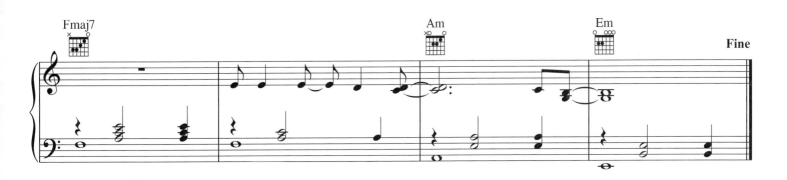

PEACHES

Words and Music by JUSTIN BIEBER,
BERNARD HARVEY, LOUIS BELL, FELISHA KING,
ASHTON SIMMONDS, ANDREW WATT, GIVEON EVANS,
LUIZ MANUEL MARTINEZ JR., AARON SIMMONDS,
KEAVAN YAZDANI and MATTHEW LEON

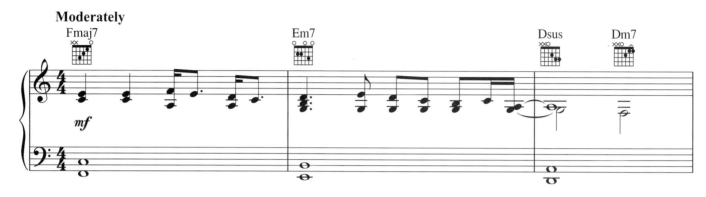

SAVE YOUR TEARS

Words and Music by ABEL TESFAYE,
MAX MARTIN, JASON QUENNEVILLE,
OSCAR HOLTER and AHMAD BALSHE

Moderate Pop

I saw you danc - ing in a crowd - ed room. You look so hap -

- py when I'm not with you. But then you saw ____ me, caught you by sur - prise,

a sin - gle tear - drop fall - ing from your eye. I don't know

SHY AWAY

Words and Music by
TYLER JOSEPH

Bright Rock, in 2

When I get __

__ home, __ you bet- ter not __ be there. __ We're plac - ing bets __

SOLAR POWER

Words and Music by ELLA YELICH-O'CONNOR
and JACK ANTONOFF

* *Recorded a half step lower. Guitar chords are in original key.*

WITHOUT YOU

Words and Music by BLAKE SLATKIN,
OMER FEDI, BILLY WALSH
and CHARLTON HOWARD

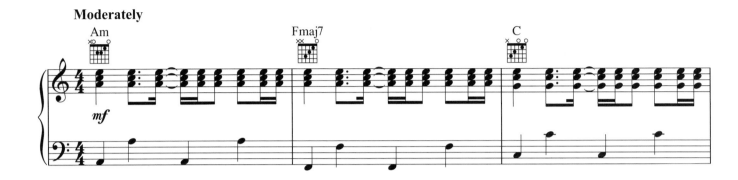

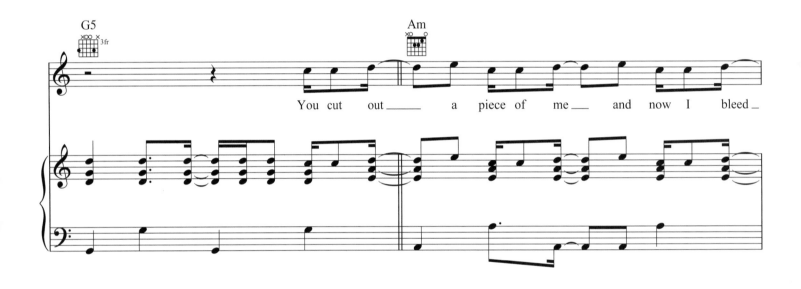

You cut out ___ a piece of me ___ and now I bleed ___

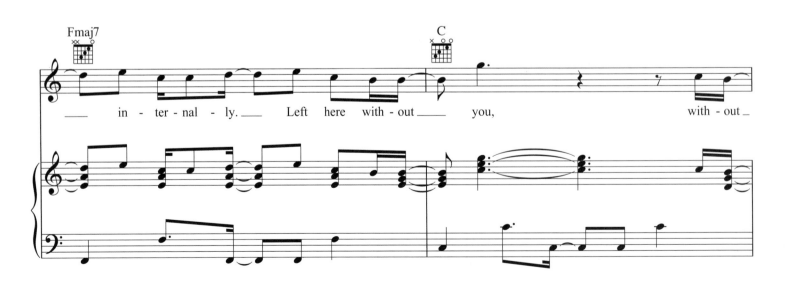

___ in- ter- nal- ly. ___ Left here with- out ___ you, with- out ___

CONTEMPORARY HITS
FOR PIANO, VOICE AND GUITAR

ALTERNATIVE ROCK SHEET MUSIC COLLECTION

40 enduring hits: Bittersweet Symphony (The Verve) • How You Remind Me (Nickelback) • Losing My Religion (R.E.M.) • Radioactive (Imagine Dragons) • Seven Nation Army (White Stripes) • Use Somebody (Kings of Leon) • We Are Young (fun.) • and more.
00356431... $24.99

BEST MODERN CHRISTMAS SONGS

20 songs: Christmas Lights (Coldplay) • Christmas Tree Farm (Taylor Swift) • Cozy Little Christmas (Katy Perry) • Everyday Is Christmas (Sia) • Glittery (Kacey Musgraves) • Hallelujah (Carrie Underwood & John Legend) • I Need You Christmas (Jonas Brothers) • Light of the World (Lauren Daigle) • Santa Tell Me (Ariana Grande) • Underneath the Tree (Kelly Clarkson) • and more.
00367424... $17.99

CHART HITS OF 2019-2020

18 top singles arranged for piano and voice with guitar chords and lyrics. Songs include: Circles (Post Malone) • Dance Monkey (Tones and I) • Everything I Wanted (Billie Eilish) • Lose You to Love Me (Selena Gomez) • Lover (Taylor Swift) • Truth Hurts (Lizzo) • and more.
00334217... $19.99

CHART HITS OF 2020-2021

20 top hits: Drivers License (Olivia Rodrigo) • Dynamite (BTS) • Ice Cream (BLACKPINK & Selena Gomez) • Kings & Queens (Ava Max) • Monster (Shawn Mendes & Justin Bieber) • Therefore I Am (Billie Eilish) • Watermelon Sugar (Harry Styles) • Willow (Taylor Swift) • and more..
00364284... $19.99

CONTEMPORARY R&B HITS

This collection pays tribute to two dozen of the best modern hits. Includes: All the Stars (Kendrick Lamar/SZA) • Girl on Fire (Alicia Keys/Nicki Minaj) • Love on the Brain (Rihanna) • Redbone (Childish Gambino) • and more.
00276001... $19.99

Order today at **halleonard.com**

EDM SHEET MUSIC COLLECTION

37 hits from the EDM genre includes: Closer (The Chainsmokers feat. Halsey) • It Ain't Me (Kygo & Selena Gomez) • The Middle (Zedd, Maren Morris & Grey) • This Is What You Came For (Calvin Harris feat. Rihanna) • Titanium (David Guetta feat. Sia) • Wake Me Up! (Avicii) • and more.
00280949... $19.99

HIT TV & MOVIE SONGS

30 songs: The Book Thief • Can't Stop the Feeling (from *Trolls*) • Downton Abbey • Finding Dory • Heathens (from *Suicide Squad*) • Light of the Seven (from *Game of Thrones*) • See You Again (from *Furious 7*) • Warm Kitty (from *The Big Band Theory*) • Writing's on the Wall (from *Spectre*) • and more.
00195514... $16.99

LATIN POP HITS

25 hot contemporary Latin songs including: Ahora Dice (Chris Jeday) • Bailando (Enrique Iglesias) • Despacito (Luis Fonsi & Daddy Yankee) • Échame La Culpa (Luis Fonsi & Demi Lovato) • Havana (Camila Cabello) • La Tortura (Shakira) • Súbeme La Radio (Enrique Iglesias) • and more.
00276076... $17.99

POPULAR SHEET MUSIC: 2017-2019

Play your favorite contemporary hits with this collection. Includes 30 songs: Bad Liar • Good As Hell • Havana • If I Can't Have You • Lover • The Middle • New Rules • Shallow • Shape of You • Sucker • Without Me • You Are the Reason • and more.
00345915... $22.99

HAL•LEONARD®

TOP CHRISTIAN HITS OF 2020-2021

20 powerful and popular songs: The Blessing (Kari Jobe & Cody Carnes) • God So Loved (We the Kingdom) • Graves Into Gardens (Elevation Worship) • Hold on to Me (Lauren Daigle) • I Will Fear No More (The Afters) • Peace Be Still (Hope Darst) • There Was Jesus (Zach Williams feat. Dolly Parton) • and more..
00364148... $19.99

TOP COUNTRY HITS OF 2019-2020

18 songs: The Bones (Maren Morris) • God's Country (Blake Shelton) • Look What God Gave Her (Thomas Rhett) • Old Town Road (Remix) (Lil Nas X feat. Billy Ray Cyrus) • One Thing Right (Marshmello & Kane Brown) • Rainbow (Kacey Musgraves) • 10,000 Hours (Dan + Shay feat. Justin Bieber) • and more.
00334223... $17.99

TOP HITS OF 2020

20 of 2020's best: Adore You (Harry Styles) • Before You Go (Lewis Capaldi) • Cardigan (Taylor Swift) • Daisies (Katy Perry) • I Dare You (Kelly Clarkson) • Level of Concern (twenty one pilots) • No Time to Die (Billie Eilish) • Rain on Me (Lady Gaga feat. Ariana Grande) • Say So (Doja Cat) • and more..
00355551... $19.99

TOP HITS OF 2021

18 of the year's best: Bad Habits (Ed Sheeran) • Beautiful Mistakes (Maroon 5 feat. Megan Thee Stallion) • Beggin' (Maneskin) • good 4 u (Olivia Rodrigo) • Leave the Door Open (Bruno Mars & Anderson Paak) • Levitating (Dua Lipa) • Peaches (Justin Bieber feat. Daniel Caesar & Givéon) • Save Your Tears (The Weeknd) • Without You (The Kid Laroi) • Your Power (Billie Eilish) • and more.
00380166... $19.99

TRENDING WORSHIP SONGS

27 contemporary worship songs The Blessing • Build My Life • Holy Water • King of Kings • Living Hope • Nothing Else • Raise a Hallelujah • See a Victory • Way Maker • Who You Say I Am • and more.
00346008... $17.99